Chocolate Fondue

MUD PUDDLE BOOKS, INC.
New York, New York

Chocolate Fondue

© 2004
By Mud Puddle Books, Inc.

Published by
Mud Puddle Books, Inc.
54 W. 21st Street
Suite 601
New York, NY 10010
info@mudpuddlebooks.com

ISBN: 1-59412-054-4

Printed in China.

Book designed by Mulberry Tree Press

Cover designed by Michelle Gengaro

Contents

Chocolate Facts 5
Fondue Facts 19
Dipping Tips 23

Sweet Chocolate Fondue 27
White Chocolate Fondue 28
Chocolate Pudding Fondue 29
Velvety Chocolate Almond Fondue 30
Chocolate Dipped Strawberries 31
White Chocolate Dipped Strawberries 32
Chocolate Maple Dipped Fruit Fondue 33
Tropical Fruit Chocolate Fondue 34
Chocolate Peanut Butter Fondue 36
Chocolate Chunky Peanut
    Butter Fondue 37
Fudgy Chocolate Fondue 38
Chocolate Fantasy Fondue 39
Chocolate-Chocolate (and more
    chocolate) Fondue 40
Toblerone® Chocolate Fondue 41
Zebra Fondue 42

Oven-Cooked Orange
    Chocolate Fondue 43
Sweet & Tart Apple Chocolate Fondue 44
Cherry Chocolate Fondue 45
Chocolate Raspberry Fondue 46
Mint Chocolate Fondue 47
Microwave Mint Chocolate Fondue 48
Orange Chocolate Fondue 49
Fiery Chocolate Caramel Fondue 50
Rum Chocolate Fondue 52
Mocha Fondue 53
Chocolate Yogurt Rum Fondue 54
Chocolate Hazelnut Fondue 55
Festive Chocolate Fondue 56
Pirates' Chocolate Fondue 57
White Chocolate Coffee Fondue 58
Bittersweet Orange Chocolate Fondue 60
South of the Border Chocolate Fondue 61
Red Hot Chilies 'n Chocolate Fondue 62
Sugarless Chocolate Fondue 63
Feed-An-Army Chocolate Fondue 64

Chocolate Facts

Facts

A timeline to
the world's tastiest treat

2000 BC   It's estimated that the cacao tree evolved 4,000 years ago in the rain forests around the Amazon and Essequibo Rivers. Here the year round high temperatures and humidity combined with the high annual rainfall to produce the ideal climate for the cacao tree.

3 AD   The ancestors of the Mayan Indians brought the cacao tree out of the rain forests to the Mayans' Central American homeland (what is now Guatemala). Chocolate derives from the cacao tree seed (the cacao bean) and the word chocolate derives from the Mayan word *xocolatl* meaning "bitter water".

600   In an extraordinary mass migration, the Mayans extended their territory from the Pacific Coast to Mexico's Yucatán Peninsula where they established the first large plantations to grow cacao. The Mayans harvested, roasted, fermented and ground the seeds of the cacao tree into a paste that was mixed with water. The result was the world's first chocolate drink. The Mayans' chocolate drink, unlike ours, was bitter to the taste.

1000 Cacao beans were so highly prized that they were used as money. The cacao tree was believed to be of divine origin (in fact, the Latin name for the tree, *Theobroma Cacao*, means 'food of the gods').

1200 The Aztec civilization, centered in the higher altitudes of the Andes Mountains, conquered the Mayans and quickly adopted their taste for cacao. Because the Aztec home was not suited for the cultivation of the cacao tree, beans were acquired as tribute or through trade. Again, the bean was used as currency and the products made from the bean were luxuries only for the very wealthy.

1502   Christopher Columbus, on his
fourth voyage to the Americas,
landed at what is now Nicaragua.
He became the first European to
be introduced to the cacao bean.
Still seeking the riches of India,
Columbus had little interest in it and
even less foresight in the potential
of a cacao industry. Subsequent
European visitors report on the use
of the cacao bean as money.

1519   Cortez conquered much of Mexico.
The victorious conquistadors looted
Montezuma's palace expecting to
find much gold and silver. Instead
they found that the Aztec treasury
consisted of cacao beans.

1528   Cortez returned to Spain with
cacao beans that, because of their
perceived value, were kept hidden
in Spanish monasteries. He also
brought the utensils for making
xocolatl. *Xocolatl* was considered
too hard to pronounce and was
corrupted to *Chocolat* (later the

English corrupted this even further to *Chocolate*). Cortez decided to add sugar to the chocolate drink and created a fashionable and expensive delicacy. Chocolate drink was made available only to the extremely wealthy. For nearly 100 years Spain was able to keep this secret from the rest of Europe.

1609   The first book devoted entirely to chocolate appeared in Mexico.

1615   When Ann of Austria, the daughter of Spain's Philip II, married Louis XIII of France, she introduced the drinking of chocolate to the French court. Naturally it was in France that chocolate first earned its reputation as an aphrodisiac and first began an association with the erotic. Casanova, it was said, used chocolate and champagne to seduce the ladies. The Marquis de Sade, on the other hand, became proficient in using chocolate to disguise poisons.

1657	A Frenchman opened London's first chocolate shop. Many more followed in rapid succession. The "chocolate houses" like the already well-established "coffee houses" became gathering places (clubs) for the wealthy and business classes.
1670	Tired of endless voyages of exploration, Pedro Bravo do los Camerinos settled in the Philippines and established one of the great cacao plantations of that time.
1697	While visiting Brussels, the Mayor of Zurich first encountered chocolate. He was so enthralled with the new taste, he took some home for his friends. This was how chocolate came to Switzerland.
1704	Chocolate was introduced to Germany and immediately taxed as a luxury by Frederick I of Prussia.
1711	Emperor Charles VI moved his court from Madrid to Vienna carrying chocolate with him.

1755   While the chocolate conquest of Europe continued unabated, America didn't get to sample the joys of chocolate until this late date.

1764   The Baker Chocolate Company was established in Dorchester, Massachusetts and, for the first time, chocolate was manufactured in America. Later, the chocolate was sold under the name "Baker's Chocolate".

1780   The first machine-made chocolate was produced at a factory in Barcelona and chocolate officially became an industry. The mechanization of the Industrial Revolution changed the process of making chocolate from a hand-made one to a machine-made one. Chocolate was produced in great quantities and at a much lower cost. For the first time, the general public could afford and enjoy chocolate treats.

1819	The first Swiss chocolate factory was established.
1822	The first cacao trees were introduced to Africa as an ornamental plant on the island of Principe in the Gulf of Guinea off the West Coast. Within 50 years the cultivation of cacao expanded to the mainland.
1824	John Cadbury opened his first chocolate shop in Birmingham, England. To this day Cadbury is one the world's most famous names in chocolate manufacturing.
1828	The cacao press was invented leading to the reduction of prices and the improvement of the quality of chocolate products.
1830	J. S. Fry and Sons, British chocolate makers, developed solid chocolate bars. Later, in 1919, J.S. Fry and Sons merged with Cadbury.
1861	Richard Cadbury, one of John's sons, created the heart-shaped candy box for Valentine's Day.

1864	Johann Tobler began producing hand-made chocolates in Berne, Switzerland.
1868	John Cadbury mass-marketed the first boxes of chocolate candies.
1875	After eight arduous years of experimentation, the Swiss manufacturers Daniel Peters and Henri Nestlé found a way to combine cocoa (the powder made from the cacao bean) and cacao butter with sugar and dried (condensed) milk to produce and market the world's first milk chocolate. Four years later the two partnered to form the Nestlé Company.
1879	Rodolphe Lindt of Berne invented a method of refining chocolate by heating and rolling it for 3 days and then adding more cacao butter. This produced a chocolate that would literally melt in your mouth.

1883   Milton Hershey, a manufacturer of caramel candies, visited the Chicago International Exposition, and became fascinated with German chocolate-making machinery. Purchasing the equipment for his factory in Lancaster, PA, he began producing chocolate coatings for his caramels.

1894   Milton Hershey created the Hershey Chocolate Corporation as a division of his caramel business. His manufacturing began to include breakfast cocoa, sweet chocolate and baking chocolate.

1897   The first known recipe for chocolate brownies appeared in a catalog for Sears and Roebuck.

1900   Milton Hershey sold the Lancaster Caramel Company for $1 million, retaining the rights to the chocolate division. He relocated this division to Derry Church, PA, the small town located in the heart of Pennsylvania dairy country and the town where he was born. He began to build the world's largest chocolate manufacturing plant. It was completed in 1905. In 1906 Derry Church changed its name to Hershey, PA, to honor its most famous son. It was the year he also introduced the Hershey Milk Chocolate Bar.

1907   Hershey's Kisses were first intro-duced.

1908   Theodor Tobler, the son of Johann Tobler, developed a triangular nougat filled chocolate bar marketed as Toblerone. Also, the Hershey Chocolate Company made the first milk chocolate bar with almonds.

1910   Switzerland established itself as the world's foremost chocolate maker winning many prizes and medals from international exhibitions.

1912   The Whitman Company began selling boxed assortments of chocolates called Whitman's Samplers. For the first time, a box came with a drawing illustrating where the different chocolates were.

1913   The Swiss position was enhanced by Jules Sechaud of Montreux who invented a process for filling chocolates.

1919   Continuing a trend started by Queen Victoria in the late 19th century when she would send her soldiers gifts of chocolate for Christmas, chocolate was part of every U.S. soldier's rations beginning with World War I. Wherever the U.S. soldier went, the popularity of chocolate skyrocketed.

1920   While visiting a local drugstore with his son Forrest, Frank Mars had an idea of producing a chocolate, malted milk bar to sell along side his line of butter-cream candies. The bar became the Milky Way bar (known in Europe as the Mars bar) and was an immediate success.

1921 Hershey's began wrapping their Kisses by machine and added the distinctive flag to the wrapping. Also, Peter Paul Halijian marketed the Peter Paul Mounds bar.

1922 H. B. Reese created Reese's peanut butter cup using Hershey's milk chocolate.

1926 Godiva Company was created by Belgian chocolatier Joseph Draps.

1930 Frank Mars made the first Snickers bar.

1939 Forrest Mars partnered with Bruce Murrie to produce chocolate with a protective candy coating to prevent melting. The candy was marketed under the name M&M's. Later Bruce Murrie became the president of the Hershey Chocolate Company.

1947   Peter Paul made the first Almond Joy.

1964   Chalet Swiss Restaurant chef Konrad Egli introduced chocolate fondue, marrying chocolate and fondue forever.

Fondue
Facts

➤ Fondue is a Swiss invention.

➤ Food produced in the summer had to last through the long, cold winters. As the weeks went by bread and cheese became as hard as bricks.

➤ The Swiss found that the cheese would become soft and edible again if it were heated with a little wine. It became customary for communities to sit around a fire, melting cheese and dipping stale bread and whatever else was available into the cheese.

➤ The name fondue comes from the French verb "fonder" meaning to melt or blend.

➤ The French vineyard owners of Burgundy adapted fondue as a convenient means of feeding their grape pickers who spent long days in the fields away from a central dining area. Fondue pots filled with oil were placed throughout the fields and workers could dunk and cook meat at their leisure without having to leave the area where they were working. This meat fondue has evolved into the classic Fondue Bourguignonne.

➤ The popularity and evolution of fondue led to its appearance in the writings of Brillat-Savarin (1755–1826), the French connoisseur and perhaps the first celebrity chef.

➤ It wasn't, however, until 1956 that the popularity of fondue really soared. It was in that year that Konrad Egli, the chef of New York's Chalet Swiss Restaurant, started a fondue craze that continues today by introducing a method of cooking meat cubes in hot oil. He followed in 1964 with the first Chocolate Fondue.

Dipping Tips

Each recipe contains recommendations for dipping. However, you should feel free to use whatever seems tasty to you.

Some suggestions for recipes that call for assorted fresh fruit are:

Whole strawberries
Banana chunks
Pineapple spears
Apricot halves
Peach slices
Pear slices
Kiwi slices
Mandarin orange segments
Tangerine segments
Seedless grapes
Pitted cherries
Mango slices
Papaya slices

Remember to pat fruit dry and brush apple and banana with lemon juice to prevent discoloring.

Recipes

Sweet Chocolate Fondue

INGREDIENTS
6 squares of unsweetened chocolate
1 cup (240 mL) light cream
1½ cups (350 mL) sugar
½ cup (120 mL) butter
1 dash salt
2 tsp (10 mL) vanilla extract

Combine all ingredients except the vanilla extract in a saucepan. Using a medium flame heat, stirring occasionally, until the chocolate is melted. Reduce heat and continue cooking for about five minutes, stirring constantly, until the mixture has thickened. Add the vanilla extract and mix well. Pour mixture into a fondue pot and serve.

DIPPING SUGGESTIONS
Assorted fresh fruit
Pound Cake cubed
Angel Food Cake cubed
Banana Bread cubed
Assorted cookies

Serves 6

White Chocolate Fondue

INGREDIENTS
12 ounces (340 g) white chocolate
1 ounce (30 mL) cherry brandy
8 ounces (240 mL) heavy whipping cream

Combine chocolate and cream in a double boiler. Heat on a medium flame, stirring constantly until chocolate is completely melted and smooth. Add cherry brandy and mix thoroughly. Pour into fondue pot and serve.

DIPPING SUGGESTIONS
Assorted fresh fruit
Pound Cake cubed
Angel Food Cake cubed

Chocolate Pudding Fondue

INGREDIENTS
  1 box chocolate pudding*
  2 cups milk (475 mL), for pudding

  * Use "regular" pudding, not "instant".

Make pudding with 2 cups (475 mL) milk
according to package directions. Pour
pudding into fondue cup.

DIPPING SUGGESTIONS
  Bananas cut into bite-sized chunks
  Shredded coconut in a bowl

Suggestion: Spear banana with fork, dip into
hot pudding, then dip into coconut.

Serves 4

Velvety Chocolate Almond Fondue

INGREDIENTS

    14 ounces (400 g) milk chocolate broken
      into pieces
    3 ounces (85 g) white chocolate, chopped
    7 ounces (200 g) marshmallow crème
    ¾ cup (175 mL) whipping cream*
    ¼ cup (60 g) finely chopped toasted
      almonds
    3 tbsp (45 mL) amaretto (optional)

  * You may substitute light cream or half-and-
    half, if desired.

Combine milk chocolate, white chocolate, marshmallow crème, whipping cream and almonds in a 4-quart (3.75 L) cooker. Cover and cook until the chocolate melts. Stir until smooth. Stir in the amaretto, if desired. Pour into fondue pot and serve.

DIPPING SUGGESTIONS

    Assorted fresh fruit
    Pound Cake cubed

Chocolate Dipped Strawberries

INGREDIENTS
- 1 cup (225 g) semi-sweet chocolate chips*
- ½ cup (115 g) milk chocolate chips*
- 1 tbsp (15 mL) shortening**
- 2 pints (900 g) fresh strawberries rinsed and patted dry

  * You may use all semi-sweet or all milk chocolate chips if you choose.
** Do not use butter, margarine or oil.

Place chocolate chips and shortening in a microwave safe bowl. Microwave at high (100%) for 1 minute. Stir. If necessary, microwave additional 30 seconds or until chips are melted and mixture becomes smooth when stirred vigorously. Hold each strawberry by the top and dip bottom ⅔ of each strawberry into the melted mixture. Shake gently to remove excess. Place on prepared tray covered with wax paper. Cover and refrigerate until coating is firm (about 1 hour).

Tip: for best results, use within 24 hours.

Makes about 3-dozen coated strawberries.

White Chocolate Dipped Strawberries

INGREDIENTS
   12 ounces (340 g) white chocolate chips
   2 tbsp (30 mL) vegetable shortening
   1 quart (900 g) strawberries

Melt the chocolate and the shortening in a double boiler. Keep stirring until smooth. Remove the pan from the heat and let the mixture cool. Skewer the strawberries on fondue forks and dip into the melted chocolate leaving the top portion of the strawberry visible. The strawberries may be eaten immediately or placed on a tray lined with wax paper for later. White chocolate dipped strawberries are best when eaten within a few hours.

Chocolate Maple Dipped Fruit Fondue

INGREDIENTS
- ½ cup (120 mL) maple syrup
- 3 egg whites
- ¼ cup (60 mL) cocoa
- ½ tsp (2 mL) vanilla extract

Heat the maple syrup in a small saucepan until it reaches 240° F (115°C) on a candy thermometer. In a large bowl, beat the egg whites with an electric mixer until stiff but not dry. Gradually beat in the hot syrup. Then beat in the cocoa and the vanilla. Continue beating until the mixture is smooth. Pour chocolate mixture into a fondue pot and serve.

DIPPING SUGGESTIONS
- Assorted fresh fruit
- Dried apricots or other dried fruits
- Crusty bread cubed

Serves 4

Tropical Fruit
Chocolate Fondue

INGREDIENTS

    16 ounces (450 g) milk chocolate broken up
        into small pieces
    3 ounces (85 g) cream cheese
    ¾ cup (180 mL) light cream*
    ¼ cup (60 mL) liqueur**

  * Half-and-half may be substituted.
** Such as brandy, almond, orange. Or, if you
    prefer, substitute ¼ cup (60 mL) cream for
    liqueur.

Beat cream cheese until smooth. Add light
cream while continuing to beat. Combine the
cream cheese mixture with the chocolate
pieces in a double boiler. Heat over a very low
flame. Stir continuously until the chocolate
has melted and the mixture is smooth. Stir in
the liqueur. Pour into fondue pot and serve.

DIPPING SUGGESTIONS

    Fresh, ripe tropical fruit cut into bite-size
        pieces (Such as mango, papaya,
        pineapple, mandarin orange and
        tangerine)

Pound Cake cubed
Angel Food Cake cubed

If desired, you may prepare the fruit in advance and refrigerate for up to two hours.

Serves 4

Chocolate Peanut Butter Fondue

INGREDIENTS

12 ounces (340 g) semi-sweet chocolate
    pieces
½ cup (120 mL) smooth peanut butter

In a saucepan melt chocolate over a low-flame, stirring constantly. When the chocolate has melted, stir in peanut butter. Mix until smooth. Heat until hot, pour into fondue pot and serve.

DIPPING SUGGESTIONS

Assorted fresh fruit
Marshmallows
Pound Cake cubed
Angel Food Cake cubed

Chocolate Chunky Peanut Butter Fondue

INGREDIENTS
6 ounces (170 g) semi-sweet chocolate
    pieces
½ cup (120 mL) sugar
½ cup (120 mL) milk
½ cup (120 mL) chunky peanut butter

Combine the chocolate pieces, sugar and milk in a medium saucepan. Heat on a low flame. Stir continuously until chocolate is melted. Stir in the peanut butter. When the combination is well mixed and heated through, pour into a fondue pot and serve.

DIPPING SUGGESTIONS
Assorted fresh fruit
Angel Food Cake cubed
Pound Cake cubed
Marshmallows
Assorted cookies

Serves 8

Fudgy Chocolate Fondue

INGREDIENTS
- ½ cup (120 mL) cocoa powder
- ½ cup (120 mL) butter
- ¾ cup (180 mL) sugar
- ½ cup (120 mL) evaporated milk
- 1 tsp (5 mL) vanilla extract

In a small saucepan melt butter over low heat. Remove from heat and stir in the cocoa immediately. Add sugar and evaporated milk. Cook over low heat, stirring constantly, until sugar is dissolved and the mixture is smooth. Remove from heat and stir in the vanilla. Pour into fondue pot and serve.

DIPPING SUGGESTIONS
- Assorted fresh fruit
- Marshmallows
- Pound Cake cubed
- Angel Food Cake cubed
- Assorted cookies

Serves 6

Chocolate Fantasy Fondue

INGREDIENTS

- 12 ounces (340 g) semi-sweet chocolate chips
- 14 ounces (415 mL) sweetened condensed milk
- 1 cup (240 mL) milk
- ¼ cup (60 mL) butter
- 1 tsp (5 mL) vanilla extract

Combine semi-sweet chocolate chips, sweetened condensed milk, butter and vanilla extract in a medium saucepan. Stir over medium heat until morsels are melted and mixture is smooth.

DIPPING SUGGESTIONS

Assorted fresh fruit
Pound Cake cubed
Macaroons

Chocolate-Chocolate (and more chocolate) Fondue

INGREDIENTS
   15 ounces (425 g) bittersweet chocolate,
      chopped
   3 tbsp (45 mL) unsalted butter, melted
   2 cups (475 mL) heavy cream
   ⅓ cup (80 mL) sugar

Using a double boiler, melt chocolate. Stir
until smooth and then add the butter. Mix
well. In a separate saucepan heat cream over
moderate heat until hot. Add sugar and stir
until dissolved. Add cream mixture to chocolate mixture a little at a time. Stir until well
mixed and smooth. Pour into fondue pot
and serve.

DIPPING SUGGESTIONS
   Assorted fresh fruit
   Assorted cookies

Serves 8

Toblerone® Chocolate Fondue

INGREDIENTS

12 ounces (340 g) Toblerone® chocolate*
broken into pieces
1 cup (240 mL) light cream**
1 tsp (5 mL) vanilla extract

* Toblerone® is a Swiss chocolate made with honey and almond nougat available wherever chocolate is sold. You may substitute 12 ounces (340 g) of semisweet chocolate chips, if desired.
** Half-and-half may be substituted.

Combine the chocolate pieces and the cream in a saucepan. Over a low heat, melt the chocolate, stirring occasionally until the mixture is smooth. Stir in the vanilla extract. Pour into fondue pot and serve.

DIPPING SUGGESTIONS

Assorted fresh fruit
Sponge Cake cubed
Pound Cake cubed
Marshmallows
Crusty bread cubed

Zebra Fondue

INGREDIENTS
- 6 ounces (170 g) semi-sweet chocolate chopped
- 6 ounces (170 g) white chocolate chopped
- ½ cup (120 mL) whole milk
- 2 tsp (10 mL) brandy

Melt the semi-sweet chocolate with ¼ cup (60 mL) of milk and 1 tsp (5 mL) brandy in a saucepan over a low flame. Stir continuously until smooth. In a second saucepan melt the white chocolate with ¼ cup (60 mL) of milk and 1 tsp (5 mL) brandy over a low flame. Stir continuously until smooth. If either mixture becomes too thick, add a little milk to thin. When the mixtures are smooth, combine them in a fondue pot. Don't stir for full zebra effect! Serve.

DIPPING SUGGESTIONS
- Assorted fresh fruit
- Pound Cake cubed

Serves 6

Oven-Cooked Orange Chocolate Fondue

INGREDIENTS
- 4 ounces (115 g) dark chocolate
- 4 tbsp (60 mL) milk
- 6 tbsp (90 mL) double cream
- ½ orange zest

Pre-heat oven to 425°F (220°C). Combine chocolate, milk, cream and orange zest in a pan and heat in the oven until chocolate is melted. Remove and stir until the mixture is smooth and pour into fondue pot to serve.

DIPPING SUGGESTIONS
- Orange segments
- Pound Cake cubed

Sweet & Tart Apple Chocolate Fondue

INGREDIENTS
- 8 ounces (230 g) semi-sweet chocolate finely chopped
- ⅓ cup (80 mL) heavy cream
- 2 tbsp (30 mL) rum*

  * You may substitute 1 tsp (5 mL) rum flavoring.

Gently heat cream in a heavy-bottom saucepan. Add chocolate and stir until the chocolate melts and the mixture is smooth. Stir in rum. Pour into fondue pot and serve.

DIPPING SUGGESTIONS
- Tart apple wedges such as Granny Smith or Jonathan
- Sweet apple wedges such as Delicious, Empire, MacIntosh or Braeburn

Cherry Chocolate Fondue

INGREDIENTS
    2 cups (255 g) milk chocolate chips
    3 tbsp (45 mL) heavy cream
    1 tbsp (15 mL) strong brewed coffee
    1 dash ground cinnamon
    2 tbsp (30 mL) cherry brandy

In a saucepan combine chocolate, cream, brandy, coffee and cinnamon. Heat over a low flame, stirring occasionally, until the chocolate has melted and the mixture is smooth. Pour into a fondue pot and serve.

DIPPING SUGGESTIONS
    Assorted fresh fruit including lots of
        pitted cherries
    Assorted cookies
    Pound Cake cubed
    Pretzels

Chocolate Raspberry Fondue

INGREDIENTS
8 ounces (230 g) chocolate*
1 tbsp (15 mL) raspberry liqueur

* You may use milk or dark chocolate or you may use a combination of both.

Combine the chocolate and the liqueur in a double boiler. Slowly melt the chocolate over a medium flame, stirring occasionally. When the chocolate has melted and the mixture is smooth, pour into a fondue pot and serve.

DIPPING SUGGESTIONS
Assorted fresh fruit including lots of raspberries
Pretzels
Pound Cake cubed

Mint Chocolate Fondue

INGREDIENTS

    6 ounces (170 g) semi-sweet chocolate
      chips
    15 ounces (445 mL) sweetened condensed
      milk
    1 pint (475 mL) jar marshmallow crème
    ⅓ cup (80 mL) crushed butter mints
    ¼ cup (60 mL) milk
    2 tbsp (30 mL) crème de cacao

In saucepan combine chocolate pieces, milk, marshmallow crème and butter mints. Cook and stir over low heat until chocolate melts. Stir in milk and crème de cacao. When the mixture is smooth, pour into fondue pot and serve.

DIPPING SUGGESTIONS

    Assorted fresh fruit
    Pound Cake cubed

Serves 6

Microwave Mint Chocolate Fondue

INGREDIENTS

6 ounces (170 g) semi-sweet chocolate
  pieces
¼ cup (60 mL) butter or margarine at room
  temperature and cut into small pieces
1 cup (240 mL) miniature marshmallows
¼ cup (60 mL) milk
2 tsp (10 mL) peppermint extract

Combine semi-sweet chocolate pieces, butter
or margarine, marshmallows and milk in a 4-
cup (950 mL) glass measure. Cover loosely
and microwave on medium (50% power) 5 to
7 minutes or until mixture is thick and smooth,
stirring at 1 minute increments. Stir in peppermint extract. Pour into fondue pot and serve.

DIPPING SUGGESTIONS

Assorted fresh fruit
Pound Cake cubed

Serves 6

Orange Chocolate Fondue

INGREDIENTS
- 8 ounces (230 g) bittersweet dark chocolate, finely chopped
- ½ cup (120 mL) whipping cream
- 1 tsp (5 mL) orange rind finely grated
- ¼ cup (60 mL) pulp-free orange juice

In saucepan, heat whipping cream and orange rind over medium-high flame until cream comes to a boil. Reduce heat to low. Add chocolate to saucepan; beat until chocolate is melted. Add and beat in orange juice. When the mixture is smooth, pour into fondue pot and serve.

DIPPING SUGGESTIONS
- Assorted fresh fruit including lots of orange
- Pound Cake cubed

Serves 8

Fiery Chocolate Caramel Fondue

INGREDIENTS
  ½ cup (115 g) milk chocolate
  ¼ cup (60 mL) milk
  ¼ cup (60 mL) caramel syrup
  2 tbsp (30 mL) chopped pecans
  2 tbsp (30 mL) rum*

  * Rum should be 151-proof for flambé. Please
    use extreme caution when preparing this
    exquisite desert, particularly when adding
    rum to a hot pan and igniting the alcohol.
    Always remove the pan from the heat source
    when adding alcohol.

Soften milk chocolate in a microwave. Heat
milk in a saucepan until it's hot. Add softened
chocolate and stir until the consistency is
smooth. Pour mixture into fondue pot. Pour
the caramel into the center of the chocolate to
create a pool of caramel. When you're ready to
serve, sprinkle the rum over the top of the
chocolate. Leave a small amount of rum on
the spoon and ignite with a lighter.

Use the flaming spoon to ignite the rum on the chocolate. When the flame burns out, it's time to dip and eat.

DIPPING SUGGESTIONS
  Assorted fresh fruit
  Marshmallows
  Pound Cake cubed

Rum Chocolate Fondue

INGREDIENTS
   7 ounces (200 g) milk chocolate
   1½ tbsp (25 mL) white rum
   1 ounce (30 mL) butter
   2 tbsp (30 mL) plain yogurt
   ¼ pint (120 mL) whipping cream

Melt chocolate, butter and rum together in a pan on low heat stirring occasionally. When the mixture is smooth, remove from heat and stir in yogurt and cream. Pour into fondue pot and serve.

DIPPING SUGGESTIONS
   Assorted fresh fruit
   Pound Cake cubed
   Banana Bread cubed
   Marshmallows

Mocha Fondue

INGREDIENTS
- 4 ounces (115 g) milk chocolate broken into pieces
- 4 ounces (115 g) semi-sweet chocolate, chopped
- ⅔ cup (160 mL) light cream or milk
- ½ cup (120 mL) powdered sugar, sifted
- 1 tsp (5 mL) instant coffee crystals
- 2 tbsp (30 mL) coffee liqueur

Combine chocolates, cream, sugar and instant coffee in a heavy saucepan. Heat over a low flame. Stir continuously until mixture is melted and smooth. Remove from heat and stir in liqueur. Pour into a fondue pot and serve.

DIPPING SUGGESTIONS
- Assorted fresh fruit
- Assorted cookies

Chocolate Yogurt Rum Fondue

INGREDIENTS
    7 ounces (200 g) milk chocolate
    1½ tbsp (25 mL) rum (white)
    1 ounce (30 mL) butter
    2 tbsp (30 mL) Greek yogurt*
    ¼ pint (120 mL) whipping cream
        (double cream)

    * Greek yogurt is especially creamy and may
      be obtained from specialty food stores or
      from websites that specialize in gourmet
      or ethnic foods.

Combine chocolate, butter and rum together in
a saucepan. Heat on a low flame until the ingredients are well mixed and hot. Remove from
heat and stir in yogurt and cream. When mixture is smooth, pour into fondue pot and serve.

DIPPING SUGGESTIONS
    Assorted fresh fruit
    Pound Cake cubed
    Banana Bread cubed
    Marshmallows

Serves 4

Chocolate Hazelnut Fondue

INGREDIENTS
- 8 ounces (230 g) bittersweet baking chocolate broken into small pieces
- ½ cup (120 mL) heavy cream
- ½ cup (120 mL) milk
- 3 tbsp (45 mL) hazelnut liqueur
- 2 tbsp (30 mL) butter, chopped

In a microwave-safe bowl, combine all fondue ingredients and wrap with plastic. Pierce a few holes in the top for steam to escape. Microwave on medium for 4 minutes, then stir the fondue mixture until smooth. Microwave on high for 1 more minute so the fondue is hot. Pour into a fondue pot and serve.

DIPPING SUGGESTIONS
- Assorted fresh fruit
- Pound Cake cubed

Festive Chocolate Fondue

INGREDIENTS
- 12 ounces (340 g) semi-sweet chocolate bits
- ⅔ cup (160 mL) sour cream
- ¼ cup (60 mL) coffee, orange, strawberry or mint liqueur
- ⅓ cup (80 mL) cream

Melt chocolate with sour cream in a heavy saucepan over a low flame. Stir constantly until smooth. Mix in liqueur. Use the cream to thin the mixture as needed. When combination is thoroughly mixed and smooth, pour into a fondue pot and serve.

DIPPING SUGGESTIONS
- Assorted fresh fruit
- Pound Cake cubed
- Angel Food Cake cubed
- Assorted cookies

Pirates' Chocolate Fondue

INGREDIENTS
  1 lb (455 g) milk chocolate, grated
  5 ounces (150 mL) light cream
  ½ tsp (3 mL) ground cinnamon
  ¼ tsp (1 mL) ground nutmeg
  3 tbsp (4 mL) dark rum
  Juice of 1 orange

In a saucepan, add cream and spices to grated
chocolate. Gently heat, stirring constantly,
until well blended. Stir in juice and rum.
Continue heating until smooth. Pour into
fondue pot and serve.

DIPPING SUGGESTIONS
  Assorted fresh fruit
  Dried apricots and/or other dried fruit
  Sponge Cake cubed
  Banana Bread cubed

Serves 6

White Chocolate Coffee Fondue

INGREDIENTS
   6 ounces (170 g) white chocolate, chopped
   ⅔ cup (160 mL) whipping cream
   2 cinnamon sticks
   ¼ cup (60 mL) coffee-flavored liqueur

Cut cinnamon sticks in half lengthwise. Break each half into smaller pieces. Combine the cream and half of the cinnamon sticks in a small saucepan. Bring to a rolling boil, remove from heat, cover and let stand for 15 minutes. Add remaining cinnamon sticks and return mixture to a rolling boil. Again, remove from heat, cover and let stand for 15 minutes. Place the white chocolate in a medium-sized bowl. Once again return the cream mixture to a boil. Immediately pour the cream mixture through a strainer into the bowl with the white chocolate. Add liqueur and stir until smooth. Pour mixture into fondue pot and serve.

DIPPING SUGGESTIONS
Assorted fresh fruit
Pound Cake cubed
Angel Food Cake cubed
Sponge Cake cubed
Assorted cookies

Bittersweet Orange Chocolate Fondue

INGREDIENTS

9 ounces (255 g) bittersweet chocolate
   broken into small pieces
½ cup (120 mL) heavy cream
2 tbsp (30 mL) orange liqueur

In a saucepan, combine the chocolate and the cream. Heat over a low flame, stirring occasionally, until chocolate has melted and the mixture is smooth. Add liqueur and stir well. Pour mixture into fondue pot and serve.

DIPPING SUGGESTIONS

Assorted fresh fruit
Pound Cake cubed
Angel Food Cake cubed
Assorted cookies

South of the Border Chocolate Fondue

INGREDIENTS
7 ounces (200 g) finely chopped Mexican
chocolate*
1 tbsp (15 mL) unsalted butter
6 tbsp (90 mL) whipping cream

* Available at specialty food shops or through
websites specializing in gourmet or Mexican
food. Mexican chocolate is traditionally made
from dark, bitter chocolate mixed with sugar
and cinnamon. Occasionally nuts are added.
Mexican chocolate is grainy and less smooth
than most chocolates. It generally comes in
disks rather than bars.

Combine cream, chocolate and butter in a
double boiler. Heat on a medium flame until
melted and smooth, stirring constantly. Pour
into a fondue bowl and serve.

DIPPING SUGGESTIONS
Assorted fresh fruit, particularly tropical fruit
Pound Cake cubed
Assorted cookies
Marshmallows

Red Hot
Chilies 'n Chocolate
Fondue

INGREDIENTS
1 medium-sized bar of dark or bittersweet
   chocolate
2 dried habanero chilies

Bring a cup of water to a boil, toss in the
habanero chilies and cover for 10 minutes or
so until the chilies are very soft. Remove the
chilies from the water, chop them very fine
and then mash them to a pulp. Melt chocolate
in a double boiler over a medium flame, stirring constantly until the chocolate is smooth.
Add the habanero pulp, stir and continue
heating. Once the chocolate is thick and
creamy, pour into a fondue pot and serve.

DIPPING SUGGESTIONS
Fresh strawberries
Pound Cake cubed

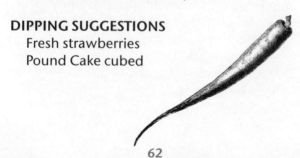

Sugarless Chocolate Fondue

INGREDIENTS
- ⅔ cup (160 mL) unsweetened cocoa powder
- ¼ tsp (1 mL) cinnamon
- 1 cup (237 mL) skim milk
- ½ tsp (3 mL) vanilla extract*
- ½ cup (60 mL) granulated sugar substitute

* You may use almond extract, if desired.

Combine cocoa powder, cinnamon and milk in a heavy saucepan. Heat over a medium flame and stir until the mixture is smooth and there are no lumps of cocoa. Bring the mixture to a boil and then lower the heat. Boil gently for five minutes stirring frequently until the mixture is smooth and thick. Allow to cool and then stir in the vanilla and sugar substitute. Pour into fondue pot and serve.

DIPPING SUGGESTIONS
Assorted fresh fruit

Serves 8

Feed-An-Army Chocolate Fondue

INGREDIENTS

32 ounces (910 g) milk chocolate, grated
1¼ cups (300 mL) heavy cream
1 tsp (5 mL) vanilla extract
1 tsp (5 mL) white sugar
⅓ cup (80 mL) hot water
1 tbsp (15 mL) instant coffee crystals*

* May be omitted, if desired.

Over a medium heat melt chocolate with the heavy cream in a saucepan, stirring occasionally. When the chocolate is melted, stir in the instant coffee, vanilla extract, sugar and hot water. Continue to heat, stirring frequently, until the mixture is smooth.
Pour into a fondue pot and serve.

DIPPING SUGGESTIONS

Assorted fresh and dried fruit
Pretzels
Assorted cookies
Pound Cake cubed
Angel Food Cake cubed

Serves 48